PAST AND PRESENT

REFUGEES

CAROLE SEYMOUR-JONES

NEW YORK

First American publication 1992 by New Discovery Books,
Macmillan Publishing Company, 866 Third Avenue, New York, NY 10022

Macmillan Publishing Company is part of the Maxwell Communication Group of Companies.

First published in 1992 by Heinemann Children's Reference,
a division of Heinemann Educational Books Ltd., Halley Court,
Jordan Hill, Oxford OX2 8EJ

Devised and produced by Zoe Books Limited
15 Worthy Lane, Winchester, SO23 7AB, England

Edited by Charlotte Rolfe
Picture research by Faith Perkins
Designed by Julian Holland

Printed in Hong Kong

Library of Congress Cataloging-in-Publication Data
Seymour-Jones, Carole.
       Refugees/Carole Seymour-Jones.
          p.   cm. — (Past and present)
       Includes index.
       Summary: Presents the history of refugees and their struggle to find homes in new lands.
       ISBN 0-02-735402-4
       1. Refugees — History — Juvenile literature. [1. Refugees — History.]
       I. Title. II. Series: Past and present. N.Y.
       JV6346.R4S49   1992
       325'.21'09 — dc20   92-14803

Photographic acknowledgments

The authors and publishers wish to acknowledge with thanks, the following photographic sources:
Mary Evans Picture Library pp 6; 7: FORMAT Partners Photo-Library pp16 (Brenda Prince); 35 (Jenny Matthews): Magnum pp 4 (Henri Cartier-Bresson); 12 (Hoepker); 15 (S.Salgado Jr.); 20 (Gideon Mendel); 28 (Chris Steele-Perkins); 37 (Raghu Rai): Peter Newark's American Pictures pp 9; 30: Popperfoto pp 19; 24; 26; 39; 41; 44: Topham Picture Source pp title page; 22

Cover photograph courtesy of Magnum/M. Erwitt

Title page: **In 1947, India's borders changed when Pakistan was created as an independent Muslim state. Over nine million people found that they were on the wrong side of the border and were forced to leave their homes. Refugees traveled in both directions — Muslims moved to the area that became Pakistan and non-Muslims left this area to live in India.**

CONTENTS

LEAVING IT ALL BEHIND

The devastation of World War II forced millions of Europeans to become refugees. Any form of makeshift transportation was used to carry their few remaining possessions.

Television cameras give us a brief glimpse into life in a makeshift camp. They scan the anxious faces at a border crossing. The **refugees** we see are only a tiny proportion of the 20 million people who roam the seas, deserts, and mountains in need of help. They are the displaced people of the twentieth century who have fled their homes because of war, poverty, starvation, or because their government persecutes them for having unacceptable religious or political beliefs.

There are refugees in every corner of the world today. In the Middle East, Palestinians have faced the misery of camp life for 40 years; in the Far East, thousands of Vietnamese have tried to escape to a new life in the West via Hong Kong. In Africa, drought has brought famine to war-torn countries and people have left their villages in search of food. In Central America, political conflict in several countries has driven people from their homes to seek shelter in camps.

The numbers of refugees have never been greater. In Africa alone, there are now officially 6 million refugees, and 2.5 million people were displaced between 1948 and 1967 in what is now Israel. In El Salvador and Guatemala over a million people have fled government death squads in fear for their lives.

A PROBLEM OF OUR TIME?

The refugee problem is not a new one. There have been refugees since earliest times. Natural disasters like plague, flood, and famine have driven people from their homes. War and conflict have also played their part.

In the thirteenth century, the great Mongol emperor Genghis Khan swept south into China from the plains of central Asia, followed by his armies of horsemen. People fled before the terrifying Mongol hordes as they crushed the towns and villages along the way. By 1214, they had conquered the ancient city of Peking, now Beijing. Genghis Khan founded an enormous empire that stretched westward from China to southern Russia. He and his successors conquered famous cities such as Kiev and Baghdad. People fled from these places into the wild

In 1492 the Roman Catholic rulers of Spain gained control of Granada, the last of the independent Muslim kingdoms in Spain. They tried to force the people to become Christians. Although the Muslims rebelled, they were defeated and given the choice of becoming Christians or leaving Spain.

and harsh countryside in the hope of escaping death or imprisonment. Their numbers may not have been as great as today, but they suffered in much the same way as the refugees of more recent times.

A WORD AND ITS STORY

The word *refugee* first came into the English language in 1685, when groups of French Protestants called *Huguenots* started arriving in England. The French king, Louis XIV, who was Roman Catholic, would no longer allow the Huguenots to practice their faith, so they fled to Protestant England. They were called "refugees" from the French verb *réfugier*, which means "to take refuge, or to seek shelter."

In 1685, after 160 years of persecution for their faith, French Protestants, or Huguenots, were finally deprived of all their religious freedom. Thousands fled to England and many were employed as silk weavers in the poor areas of London.

The Huguenots chose to live in England, a foreign country, because there they could go to church as they wished, and also work freely. In France many jobs were closed to Protestants so that it was difficult for them to earn a living. They knew that if they held Protestant church services they risked going to prison, and they even feared for their lives. Reasons like this still force people to leave their own homes today.

By 1780 the word *refugee* had crossed the Atlantic to the United States. There it was used to describe fleeing supporters of the English king, George III, in the War of Independence against England.

MILLIONS ON THE MOVE
World War I (1914 – 1918) brought a flood of refugees in its wake. The League of Nations was set up after the war, and in 1921 it appointed the Norwegian explorer and

statesman Dr. Fridtjof Nansen as high commissioner for refugees. He was faced with many different problems. There were large numbers of Armenians and Greeks who had fled from armies in the newly founded republic of Turkey. There were nearly 1.3 million Russians escaping from famine in south Russia after revolution and **civil war**, and 500,000 German and Austro-Hungarian prisoners of war to be brought home. Nansen invented a special passport to help **stateless** people with no national documents to travel in safety.

World War II (1939 – 1945) caused still more waves of refugees to wander across the map of Europe. Ten million people were displaced after Nazi Germany's defeat in 1945.

In the years following the war, the newly formed United Nations Organization (UNO) set out a new definition of refugees and also created the United Nations High Commission for Refugees (UNHCR) to protect displaced persons.

A refugee is someone who "owing to a well-founded fear of being persecuted for reasons of race, religion, nationality, membership of a particular social group or political opinion is outside the country of his nationality and is unable or, owing to such fear, is unwilling to avail himself of the protection of that country."

UN Convention on the Status of Refugees, 1951

It was agreed that refugees should not be forced to return home if this would place them in danger of persecution. Refugees have the right to apply for **asylum** and to show the political nature of their plight according to agreed conditions. While their cases are being examined they should be treated fairly.

The root causes that drive people to flee their native country continue to flourish today in many places. Unlike **emigrants**, refugees do not choose to go to another country. They go because they feel they have no other choice.

FORCED TO FLEE

The forcible removal of the Cherokee Indians in 1838.
Inadequate food supplies and freezing weather caused
terrible suffering. Many Indians died on the 116-day journey
along the "Trail of Tears."

In the eighteenth century, the idea of "human rights" common to all people was expressed by philosophers like the French writer Jean-Jacques Rousseau (1712 – 1778). His comment on the injustices of his time has since become famous: "Man is born free, and everywhere he is in chains." In the French Revolution of 1789, the cry was for "liberty, equality, fraternity." People have fought for the freedom of speech and the freedom to hold political or religious beliefs without persecution in many countries throughout the ages. Sadly, these freedoms are not allowed in two thirds of the countries of the world today. **Human rights** violations are still one of the main causes of refugee movements across national borders.

THE FLIGHT FROM EGYPT

Perhaps one of the most famous refugee stories describes the escape of the Israelites from Egypt. It is certainly one of the earliest refugee journeys ever recorded.

Over 3,000 years ago, in about 1280 B.C., the Egyptian pharaoh, or ruler, treated the Israelites as slaves because he was alarmed at the way their population was growing. The Israelites were a nomadic people who had settled in Egypt for 400 years and led a relatively comfortable life, until the pharaoh set taskmasters over them and forced them to build him treasure cities; their lives "were bitter with hard bondage," as the Bible explains. Finally he ordered that all their baby boys should be killed.

It was not only their life of slavery that persuaded the Israelites to leave Egypt; they also believed that their God, Jehovah, wanted them to return to the land of Canaan or Palestine, "a land flowing with milk and honey," which he had promised them. It was this belief in God's destiny for them that encouraged them to follow their leader Moses, despite the threats of famine and death in the wilderness of the Sinai desert.

Like many decisions to flee, this had more than one cause. There are usually **"push and pull" factors** that combine to influence people's decisions to leave. For the Israelites the freedom to practice their religion in a homeland of their own was an important "pull" factor.

"TRAIL OF TEARS"

Sometimes people are pushed out of their own homes by another more powerful group. The struggle for land has been the cause of conflicts today and in the past. In the Americas many native peoples became refugees in their own country, as Europeans moved in with different ideas about land use and ownership.

The North American Cherokee Indians lived in and around the southern Appalachian Mountains. They lived in small villages and practiced agriculture. They adopted new farming techniques and developed cotton and wool industries from the early European settlers in the area, and they had their own government. During the 1830s however, they lost huge amounts of land to the settlers in various treaties — the worst of which was the Treaty of New Echota (1835). Under this agreement, they were required to leave the land within three years. Although most Cherokee rejected the treaty, they were herded into camps and their homes were burned. During the winter of 1838 – 1839 they were marched by force to Indian Territory (now part of Oklahoma), over 600 mi (967 km) away. More than 15,000 Cherokee men, women, and children made the journey, with little or nothing in the way of protection against hunger and the cold weather. About 4,000 of them died on the way. Even the American soldiers guarding them described the conditions as terrible, and the journey became known as the "Trail of Tears."

KEEPING PEOPLE IN

People may also be stopped from traveling outside their country. A government may use its power to keep people within the country by not allowing them the necessary papers to travel — a passport, for example. Those found trying to cross the border illegally may be imprisoned or even executed. This kind of restriction on travel has been used in many countries, especially those where the government abuses human rights in order to keep itself in power.

When war breaks out between rival powers within a

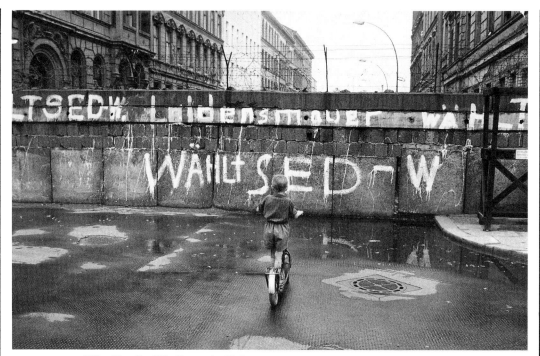

The Berlin Wall was built in 1961 to stop skilled workers from the East crossing to prosperous West Germany. Originally it was a barbed-wire barricade, but by 1980 the wall was 10 feet (3.5 m) high and more than 850 mi (1,368 km) long.

single country, the usual "escape" routes such as ports and airports are quickly closed. People may be forced to find other ways of reaching safety. During the Spanish Civil War (1936 – 1939) over half a million refugees fled across the Pyrenees Mountains into France.

People living in one country may also want the freedom and improved living conditions they believe they can have somewhere else. This is what happened during the 1950s in Communist East Germany. The escape route here was through Berlin. At the end of World War II, Berlin was jointly occupied by the Western powers (Britain, France, and the United States) and the Communist Soviet Union.

During the twenty or so years following the war, over two million East Germans crossed into West Berlin. From here they could travel freely to resettle in West Germany or elsewhere.

Most of these people were highly skilled workers, which East Germany could ill afford to lose. By 1961 the East German government decided that direct action was needed to stop the flow. On the night of August 13, police and soldiers sealed all the borders between East and West Berlin and quickly put up a large barricade of barbed wire. Over the following days, a wall was built. It sealed East Berlin off from the West for the next 28 years.

During this time, a number of escape attempts were made. Some were successful, but 200 refugees lost their lives as they tried to cross the wall. They were shot dead by East German border guards under government orders. In 1989 the Communist government in East Germany collapsed, and the wall was finally pulled down.

DRIVING PEOPLE OUT

In many countries, there are **ethnic minority** groups who have settled for historical reasons. When Uganda became independent in 1962, there was a large Asian community living there. The Asians had originally come from India to East Africa to help build the railroads during colonial times, when the area was under British rule. Over the years they settled down with their families. Many had started businesses and had become quite prosperous. Like many minorities, however, they found that their position was not always certain, and their rights not fully protected in the newly independent state.

> Uganda was my home. I had never been anywhere else. I was ten when I left on the airplane with my mother. My father promised he would follow us in a few days. I did not know if I would ever see him again.
>
> *Asian refugee from Uganda,*
> *remembering 1972*

Early in 1971, the commander of the Ugandan army, Major-General Idi Amin, seized control of the country and ruled as a dictator for the next ten years. In 1972, he announced that all Asians would have to leave Uganda, and that their property would be taken over by African Ugandans. Over 30,000 Asian refugees fled the country. Many of those who remained behind were murdered by Amin's soldiers.

Most of the refugees had British passports that had been issued to them when Uganda had become independent. For this group that meant guaranteed entry into Britain. For the 6,500 stateless Asians, the solution was not so straightforward and some had the terrifying experience of being flown from one strange country to another in search of refuge. The international community made a great effort to resettle them, and many found new homes in the United States, Canada, and elsewhere. However, the process took many painful months.

FLIGHT FROM STARVATION

In many countries in the world, people's lives depend greatly on the animals they keep and the few crops they manage to grow. If they find themselves in the middle of a long war, as has happened to many ordinary people in Ethiopia, for example, their entire livelihood can be destroyed and they might face starvation unless they move out and search for a new chance somewhere else. If the disturbance of war combines with natural disasters such as drought, people's suffering is increased.

Although Africa has many fertile regions, the continent — which in 1960 exported more food than it imported — today needs $1 billion a year in food aid, and most African countries are on the UN list for emergency help. There are many reasons for this worsening situation, which has cost the lives of so many refugees:

- Desertification. This is partly due to drought and partly the result of people cutting down trees for firewood. The Sahara desert today gallops south at a rate of 6 mi (10 km) a year.
- High population growth. This means that more people compete for fewer resources such as agricultural land, food, and water. In less than 30 years Sudan, Kenya, and Nigeria will more than double their populations.

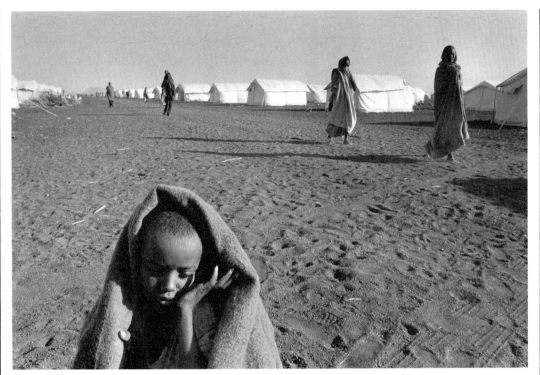

This child may spend many years in one of these temporary camps, set up to house thousands of environmental refugees who have been driven from their homeland in Ethiopia by years of famine.

- Poor road and rail connections. This makes distribution of food aid and essential agricultural supplies difficult in rural areas. (The problem is made worse when a corrupt government takes the aid that is meant for the people, or when the supply routes are attacked by warring armies.)

Refugees who leave their homes for reasons such as drought or famine are known as environmental refugees. Many of them suffer in the poorest of camps on the edge of a town or city, with no hope of ever returning and little chance of international refugee assistance.

A WARM WELCOME?

When the Communists took control of Vietnam, thousands
of people fled to Hong Kong, already a densely populated
country. To deter any further refugees, the "boat people"
were put into "closed camps." Many Vietnamese have lived
in these squalid conditions in Hong Kong for many years.

Most refugees face one main problem: Will they be welcome in the **host country** to which they flee? In poorer countries, it may not be easy to look after extra numbers of people making demands on jobs, living space, social services, and other scarce resources. Existing inhabitants of the country may feel that the new arrivals are competing with them for these things.

In the rich countries of the world, people sometimes also talk about being "swamped" by unwanted **immigrants,** especially those of a different cultural background. Newcomers may find that they are automatically blamed for many of the problems in the new country, such as housing shortages, crime, and racial tension. Small numbers of refugees with some means of supporting themselves may be welcomed into the community; but when large numbers of poor people seek refuge and a new start in life, host governments begin to react differently.

CLOSING THE DOOR IN SOUTHEAST ASIA

In 1975, the city of Saigon finally fell to the Communist forces in the last stages of the Vietnam War. Thousands of Vietnamese risked their lives to cross the sea to safety, often in small, insecure fishing boats. They were joined by people from neighboring countries such as Laos and Cambodia. These countries had also been thrown into disorder by the years of war in the region. By 1978, some 86,000 "boat people" as they became known, had arrived in Thailand and other Southeast Asian countries.

The Thai government was dismayed. Its leader, Premier Kriangsak, said that Thailand was not being "flooded" by refugees, it was being "drowned," as thousands of fare-paying Vietnamese arrived in chartered ships. The government began to **screen,** or check, arrivals, in order to find out who were "real" refugees, "with a well-founded fear of being persecuted," as the 1951 UN Convention on the Status of Refugees put it. They suspected that many people simply came in search of a better life and they labeled these people **economic refugees.**

Different countries used a variety of ways to keep newcomers out. Sometimes they sealed off borders. Malaysia used a "push-off" policy, and simply rejected more than 50,000 Vietnamese who tried to land there. Some governments demanded that newcomers should carry a **visa** — a special travel document — that they should obtain before traveling. New arrivals were sometimes sent back to the last country they had called at on their journey.

At the time, some Western countries objected to the screening of refugees, and particularly to the use of **forced repatriation,** when refugees were sent back against their will to face an unknown future in their own country. In 1979, at a meeting in Geneva, 65 countries tried to solve the problem of the boat people, and countries in the West agreed to take 250,000 of the refugees.

LIVING IN NO-MAN'S-LAND

In spite of all the difficulties, thousands of people continued to cross the border into Thailand. Some of the Thai refugee camps could clearly be seen from across the border by the people of Laos, one of the poorest countries in the world. These camps were comfortable, they were financed by international aid, and they provided better medical care than anything available to the poor people outside the camp gates. They also offered the possibility of resettlement in the United States or another country. To the war-weary people of neighboring Cambodia and Laos, it was a walk to freedom and a new life.

In order to discourage people, the Thai government set up new camps where conditions were extremely tough, and where there was no chance of resettlement. By 1982, the Hong Kong government decided to do the same with its own population of boat people, by operating "closed camps." Conditions there were not unlike the worst sort of prison — overcrowded and completely lacking in privacy.

To the people trapped in these camps, the future was uncertain. As the years went by, the dread of being sent back increased. Since 1989, groups of refugees have been regularly sent back to Vietnam. In 1989, a group of boat

In 1989 a controversial plan of forced repatriation for Vietnamese boat people was put into operation. Here Hong Kong police use force to push an unwilling refugee onto a plane bound for Hanoi, the capital of Vietnam.

people was forcibly repatriated from Hong Kong to Vietnam. People in the Hong Kong camps protested violently against this treatment, but they were silenced by riot police. Today, people are still being sent back to Vietnam, but not by force. Whatever other countries may wish, the government of Vietnam itself has refused to accept anyone who has not returned "voluntarily."

RESCUE OF A LOST PEOPLE

In other circumstances, refugees have been made welcome in the host country. For over a hundred years, the United

States took in waves of European refugees who fled to a new life from revolution and two world wars. In more recent years, Israel went one step further in rescuing the Jewish inhabitants of Ethiopia, a country devastated by war and famine.

The Falashas — as they are known (the word means "stranger") — had lived in this part of Africa for centuries. No one knows how they first came to Ethiopia, although the Falashas believe they are descended from those who returned to Africa with the Queen of Sheba after she visited Jerusalem during the tenth century B.C.

At the beginning of the twentieth century there were 100,000 Falashas in Ethiopia, but as a small, separate community they suffered at the hands of various Ethiopian governments: They were murdered, tortured, and sold into slavery. They now number only 20,000.

This Falasha grandmother, rescued from persecution in Ethiopia by "Operation Solomon," has great difficulty in adjusting to the housing and facilities in Israel, after a completely different way of life in Africa.

In 1971 the American Association for Ethiopian Jewry began the campaign for a rescue operation to remove the Falashas to safety in Israel. The first secret airlift took place in 1985. In 1991, "Operation Solomon" was mounted: 14,000 Ethiopian Jews were flown to Israel from Ethiopia's capital city, Addis Ababa. It was the biggest air rescue operation in Israeli history.

On reaching Israel, the Ethiopian refugees faced a culture shock. Within hours, they found themselves removed from a simple life of farming that had not changed much for thousands of years. They had to face the newness of modern Israeli living — with a strange diet, packaged food, Western-style housing and a language and life-style completely unknown to them.

Nevertheless, the new Ethiopian-Israelis are fortunate because they possess the documents necessary in the twentieth century world: identity cards or passports giving proof of nationality. Without these, a person is stateless, unacceptable to the countries he or she may wish to enter. If a stateless person arrives by air or sea, he or she will be turned back. Without identity papers there is no way out of a refugee camp, no means of building a new life.

> There is little historical evidence to support the argument that most refugees are deterred by the threat of inhumane treatment on arrival — which they have too often received — when the need to leave their own country has been compelling.
>
> *Dennis MacNamara, UNHCR, 1990*

HOW TO HELP?

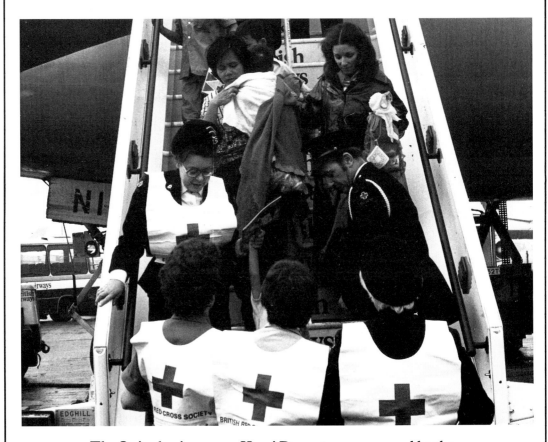

The Swiss businessman Henri Dunant was so moved by the horror of seeing thousands of wounded soldiers left to die on an Italian battlefield that he set up the first "Voluntary Aid Society" in 1863. This became the Red Cross. More than a century later, British members of this worldwide organization welcome Vietnamese refugees in London.

Since World War II, international organizations have been developed to protect refugees. The United Nations High Commission for Refugees (UNHCR) cooperates with national governments and voluntary organizations such as the Red Cross or Red Crescent, Oxfam, Christian Aid, and Save the Children Fund. These voluntary organizations claim to be nonpolitical and unbiased, nonprofit-making, and to have experience with the "grass roots," which makes them the best agencies to help displaced people. Certainly most of these organizations are sincere and well intentioned in their efforts, but it is doubtful whether they alone can solve what has become a world problem.

> Many people still attempt to approach the refugee problem. . . as if it were a charity. This attitude will never be enough to meet the problems of the 1990s.
>
> *UN High Commissioner for Refugees, 1990*

WORK OR REFUGE?

In the 1950s, Europe, struggling to recover from two wars, quickly absorbed refugees and displaced people from Central and Eastern Europe. In the 1960s Western governments had a shortage of labor, and as a result 10 million **guest workers** were recruited from southern Europe. Refugees from the dictatorships of Greece, Spain, and Portugal were easily absorbed in countries that required their labor and skills.

But as the refugee crisis in Southeast Asia showed, by the 1980s the situation had changed. In 1985, 19 million people were unemployed in Western Europe, and individual countries began to question whether they had room for large numbers of Asian immigrants. In the 1980s the total European intake of refugees for one year was 850,000, while the United States and Canada took another 700,000. In 1985 there was a turning point. For the first time the number of refugees seeking asylum was greater than the number of legally admitted foreign workers.

WHOSE AID? WHOSE INTERESTS?

Some people argue that the various organizations set up to solve the refugee problems of today are not always in a position to do what is best for the refugees. These organizations depend on the rich countries of Europe and North America, and on Japan and Australia, for their financial and political support. National interests, as we have seen, may simply be to keep people out. In many of these countries there are **racist** pressure groups or political parties who argue that people should be stopped from entering the country simply on the ground of their race or their color.

A second criticism of the refugee organizations is that they do not respond to refugee problems until too late. In the case of the Kurds who fled the Iraqis during the 1991 Gulf War, international help was slow to come. Only when the world's media has drawn attention to suffering does

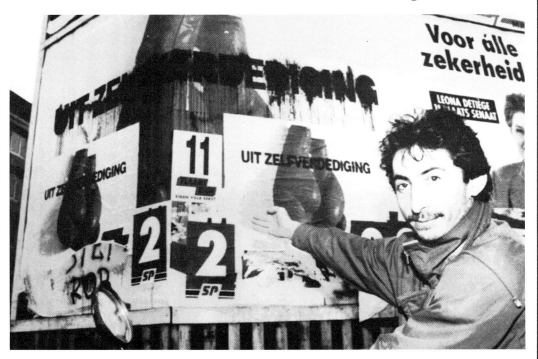

Not all immigrants are welcome in their adopted countries. This young Turkish immigrant in Belgium is pointing at an election poster for an extremist party. The slogan reads, "For self-defense. Our own people first."

the West offer financial aid. The refugee organizations themselves argue that they have learned much in the last 30 years. Instead of handouts of food and medical relief and welfare payments to refugees, they have moved into setting up development projects that have the aim of helping many people who might otherwise become environmental refugees.

THE CAMP SYSTEM: HAS ANYTHING CHANGED?

The "we know what's best for them" approach to refugees is still seen in refugee camps, which are often created for the sake of convenience. In camps it is easier to count refugees, to deliver aid, and to control food distribution. Also people and governments are more likely to give money to refugees when they are visible in camps and can be photographed than when they are settled in a host society. But what do the refugees themselves think?

> Refugees generally dislike camps and avoid them as much as possible. They tend to use them only as a "safety net" when all else fails, as support for their most vulnerable family members, or where there are security problems.
>
> *Refugee Participation Network, 1991*

A list of camp dangers might read:
1. Health risk: Camp populations are exposed to disease.
2. Unemployment: There is often no work for camp populations.
3. Dependency: Camp populations lose control over their own lives.
4. Local hostility: Local communities dislike camps in their midst, which strain local resources.
5. Integration into host country is more difficult in camps.

These dangers are well known. The 1982 *UNHCR Handbook* advises field officers to establish camps only as a last resort. Nevertheless, because refugees are so often

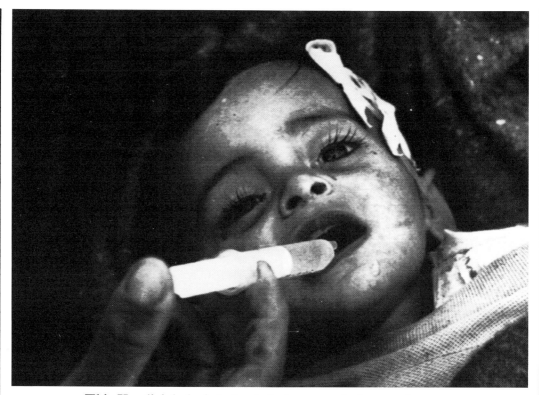

This Kurdish baby is being fed glucose to help stop the effects of dehydration. The lack of water in the Turkish refugee camps, set up after the Gulf War, has meant that many people living there suffer from dehydration.

powerless victims of circumstances, they often find themselves in camps against their will. In a survival situation they have no choice.

Since the state of Israel was founded in 1948 many Palestinian Arabs previously living in the area have ended up in refugee camps run by the United Nations Relief and Works Agency (UNRWA). In the 1948 – 1949 war between the new state of Israel and its Arab neighbors, 750,000 small landowners, farm workers, and laborers lost their homes and jobs. They fled from the territory, which became the state of Israel, to surrounding areas such as the West Bank, the Gaza Strip, and neighboring Arab countries such as Jordan, Lebanon, and Syria.

In the 1967 Arab-Israeli war, another 500,000

Palestinians lost their homes in the territories occupied by Israel. In 1988, the fortieth anniversary of the Universal Declaration of Human Rights, the Palestinians began the *intifada,* or uprising against Israeli occupation of the West Bank and Gaza Strip. The United Nations condemned Israel for "violating the human rights of Palestinian people in the occupied Palestinian territories, including Jerusalem." The Commission on Human Rights in 1988 also condemned Israel's use of violence. But although the UN recognizes the rights of the Palestinian people to govern themselves and to have national independence, its pronouncements seem to have little effect. The Palestinian **diaspora** has lasted over 40 years.

One example of life in a Palestinian camp shows what everyday life can be like. Saffiyeh Hamdan and her seven children live in Nuseirat camp, Gaza, in a two-room shelter. Her son, aged 20, is the breadwinner, bringing home about 20 shekels a day (about $10) for picking oranges for eight hours. However, if there is a curfew, he cannot work. The UNRWA gives these refugees flour and skimmed milk rations. The children fight and quarrel, as the UNRWA schools are shut while the curfew lasts. They cannot leave their home for fear of army patrols.

SKILLS TRAINING AND EDUCATION
In order to give refugees self-respect and to help them to support themselves, some organizations run training programs in refugee camps, such as Beqa'a, 12 mi (20 km) north of Amman. This is the largest Palestinian refugee camp in Jordan. Most families here do not like their wives and daughters to work outside the camp in factories, but allow them to make school uniforms, nurses' gowns, and chefs' uniforms at the vocational training center. Not only does this give them an income, it also helps them feel less dependent and isolated.

Refugees prize education as a way out of camps for their children. The UNRWA runs 631 schools for the Palestinians, and provides university scholarships. In Beqa'a camp there is a nursery school for 380 children and a program for women on health and child care and

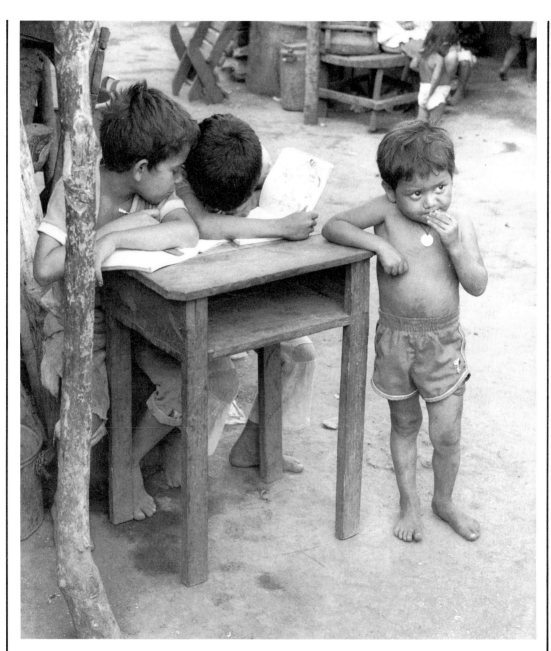

Civil war in El Salvador has made thousands homeless. Refugee camps have become permanent homes for these people. This camp near San Salvador houses 800 refugees. Although few facilities exist, education continues and these boys show that classroom habits are the same everywhere, no matter where lessons are held.

women's rights. As women and children form the majority of refugees in the world today, training and study programs have been geared toward their needs.

NO WAY OUT

In 1978 thousands of nomads fled civil war in Ethiopia. Having lost most of their herds of cattle, they were organized into 35 camps in Somalia containing over a million refugees. Being settled in one place brought dramatic changes to the life-style and diet of the nomads: instead of meat and milk they had to eat inadequate cereal rations. Diseases such as scurvy and anemia broke out, because of lack of vitamin C and iron. In one camp alone 60 women died of bleeding during childbirth due to severe anemia.

There were problems in keeping the camps clean and healthy. Diseases such as malaria and measles spread, because of overcrowding. Because the numbers of refugees were not accurately counted, it was difficult to obtain enough food from donors, who thought the figures were exaggerated and sent less food. Families who did not have "ghost members," or surplus ration cards, went short of food, especially women.

LESSONS LEARNED?

The experience of dealing with ever greater numbers of refugees, and the knowledge of conditions in long-term refugee camps, has helped many of the refugee organizations to improve their efforts and to give more appropriate support. But it is still difficult to predict a massive movement of people, or to obtain enough help in advance to deal with the problem. A flow of refugees can occur very quickly, as often happens in a war or a natural disaster. Relief organizations know that it can take many months to organize essential supplies, and that people are more at risk at certain times of the year, such as during cold winter months, or during a hot, dry season. Yet their warnings about future crises are not always heeded.

CROSSING OVER

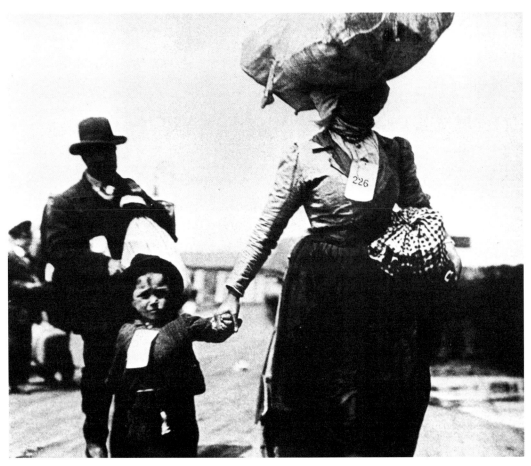

These immigrants arriving in America about 1900 were typical of the millions who sought a better life in the "land of plenty." Ellis Island, in New York City's harbor, was the nation's major immigration center from 1892 to 1943.

Losing one's home and country, friends and familiar culture through flight can feel like losing a close relative or friend through death. Feelings of great sadness and regret may mingle with anger and despair. It takes time to adjust or "cross over" to the new life, and for many the experience leaves a permanent scar.

THINKING ABOUT THE PAST

Refugees are all individuals with their own personal past or "ghost reality." This ghost reality is often the main barrier to settling down and becoming part of a new society. It can sometimes appear as an escape from the problems of coping with a new and different way of life.

One woman who fled to Australia from her island home in East Timor, Indonesia, explains how her memories of the past affected her abilities to get on with her new life:

"I survive the present by living in the past and only the future will tell me how well I have coped. . . . I was probably dreaming but it was a painful daylight dream — one about the past which is now a lost present: family, language, job, culture and country. It was a cloudy dream in which I had no sense of direction and time. Though I knew I had always been confident of my moves, this time I was losing control over my existence — I started to feel powerless and very dependent on my friends."

For many refugees, the past contains horrific memories. Fourteen-year-old May risked her life when she and her sisters left Vietnam in a refugee boat with 22 other passengers. The boat was attacked by pirates, and six women, including May and her sisters, were captured and sexually abused. May was separated from her sisters and transferred to another fishing boat. Then she was thrown into the sea, where she drifted for a day and a half before being rescued by a marine police boat and brought ashore. She has never seen her sisters again.

May told the police what had happened and was able to remember the number of the fishing boat, which led to the pirates' arrest. However, at the identification lineup she was too terrified to identify her attackers. After a seven-month waiting period in a refugee camp May settled in the

United States, but she has never had any further news of her family. She has had to make a new life alone in the world, except for the support of her counselor and the authorities.

FACING THE FUTURE

Every refugee's goal is to make a new home either in the country to which he or she flees or in another, third country. Sometimes, sadly, the halfway house of camp life becomes permanent, as it has for many Palestinians, and for over three million Afghans in Pakistan. Sometimes refugees return to their country of origin, as some Vietnamese have done. But getting out of the camps and tackling day-to-day problems is the first step along the road toward **integration** — becoming part of a new society.

FITTING IN

At various times in the sixteenth and seventeenth centuries, Protestant refugees from continental Europe sought safety in England. Although these exiles set up their own churches, like the French Protestant church in Threadneedle Street in the City of London, they soon became integrated into English society. This was partly because they brought welcome skills such as silk-weaving and glass-blowing.

Many Protestants also emigrated to North America. In 1621 Philippe de la Noye, a Huguenot, arrived at Plymouth, Massachusetts, on the *Fortune;* one of his

> The poor exiles from Flanders, France and other countries. . . are our brethren; they live not idly. If they have houses of us, they pay us rent for them. . . they beg not in our streets. . . they labour truthfully, they live sparingly. They are good examples of virtue, travail, faith and patience.
>
> *John Jewell,*
> *English bishop (1522–1571)*

descendants was Franklin D. Roosevelt. In 1629 another Huguenot, Baron de Sauce, sailed from France to Virginia where he established a settlement of Huguenots; today many Virginia families have French surnames.

During the nineteenth century and the years leading up to World War I (1914 – 1918), over 32 million people emigrated to the United States. Many were fleeing from war, persecution, or famine. After World War II (1939 – 1945), there was a further wave of refugees, mainly from Central and Eastern Europe. For most of this group, there was an important hurdle to cross: language. One young German refugee describes his experience in the early 1950s:

"My father had been killed in the war, and there was no future for us in Germany. After some time in a refugee camp, we sailed to America, where my mother got a job helping her old professor from Berlin — he had fled to America before the war. My two brothers and I stayed at a children's home, where we were separated and made to speak English from the start. I was nine years old, and I found it very hard."

Speaking the language of the host country is perhaps the most important key to integrating into its society. It helps the newcomer to deal with other challenges such as finding work and a place to live. Other factors such as race, religion, and political views also affect the way in which an individual fits into a new country. Many refugees form their own communities as a natural way of preserving their own traditions and giving each other support when necessary.

INTEGRATING IN AUSTRIA

In 1956 after the Hungarian revolution, which was crushed by the Communists, 200,000 refugees fled to Austria, and Traiskirchen became the country's main reception and **transit camp,** helping people prepare for their new lives. In 1982, 25,000 Poles also sought asylum in Traiskirchen, by then the biggest refugee camp in Europe.

Today, it provides a minimum of accommodation,

food, and free medical care for 11,000 Romanians, as well as Bulgarians and others who crossed from Eastern Europe to the West before and after the fall of the Berlin Wall in 1989. In 1990 there were over 43 nationalities in the camp. They spoke English, German, Flemish, French, Italian, Romanian, Hungarian, Iranian, Yugoslavian, Bulgarian, and Turkish.

As a result, communication is not easy. As one camp leader has noted, "Sometimes the only possible language that can be used is the body language, but one always uses the heart language." To prepare refugees for integration there are special language courses. For the many who settle in Austria, it is essential to learn German. Films are shown about the other countries to which refugees may emigrate, such as the United States, Canada, Australia, Britain, Israel, and Scandinavia.

Children may be quicker than their parents at adapting to a new culture. At Traiskirchen, they go to Austrian schools and have their own camp program of arts and crafts. Summer camps have been used for many years at Traiskirchen as a way of removing the children, for a while at least, from the tension of camp life. As the camp director wrote in 1952, "We tried. . . to make them forget for a while the disappointment and frustration of postponed emigration schemes, the overcrowding of barrack life, black marketeering, stealing etc., habits into which many of the refugees have fallen." Reconciling national groups to each other is also an important task in the camp. Different nationalities may fear and hate each other, just as they feel fear of the unknown outside the camp.

Yet these European refugees are perhaps the lucky ones, for they represent only 5 percent of refugees worldwide in 1991, and there is an efficient system in operation to help them lay at rest the ghosts of the past. Racism is not a major problem in integrating Europeans from one country into another. In the poorer countries of the Third World the picture is bleaker, the problems different, the numbers far greater. Host countries themselves may be hard-pressed to provide all the extra help needed.

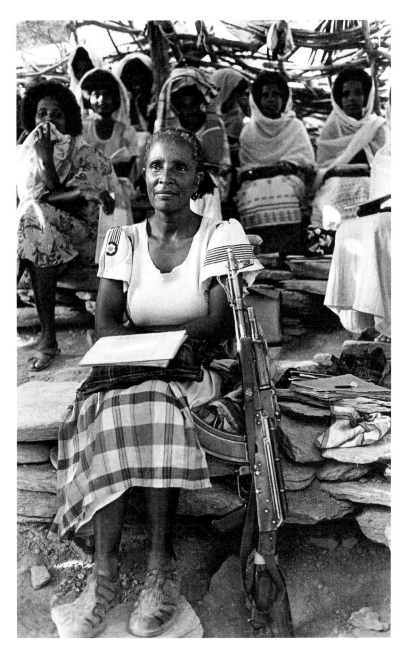

These women are being taught to read and write in a camp in Eritrea, a province of Ethiopia. Eritrea wants independence from Ethiopia and rival factions fight bitterly among themselves about the best way to achieve this. Villagers seek refuge in camps, but even during lessons, weapons stay within reach.

INTEGRATING IN SWAZILAND

Since most refugees do not want to be dependent on aid, they stay out of camps if possible. In 1984, there were 14,500 refugees from the fighting in Mozambique living in camps. The camps were isolated and jobs were scarce. Trading was difficult because the refugees were poor and the camps were far away from markets. By contrast, the large numbers of Mozambicans (estimates vary from 60,000 to 134,000) who settled in the border areas of neighboring Swaziland worked out their own ways to survive. Local villagers lent them small plots of land to cultivate and they also worked for local farmers as day laborers.

The refugees provided cheap labor for the small-scale farmers, who were able to increase production. When drought came to Swaziland in 1987, the government began a border feeding program of corn and beans for the refugees who were registered with host families. Each family was given a ration card.

However, after October 1990, the refugees were told that if they wanted to continue receiving food, they would have to move into Malindza refugee camp. The border feeding program was to be phased out at the height of the hungry season. The refugees moved to the camp unwillingly — they knew they were losing freedom and dignity and becoming dependent on handouts. Some saw Malindza as "a death trap, a place of no hope."

Local Swazi chiefs resented the fact that the food program was stopped without their agreement and the refugees were moved to the camp. They wanted the refugees to be registered so that they could keep track of their movements. "Before, the refugees were with us, under our care, but now they are under UNHCR... . How can we trust them?"

All these events in Swaziland showed how the refugees were better off when actively contributing to their own survival and working within a community. Once they were removed to a camp, they lost the trust and cooperation of the local people as well as their own freedom.

SHARING THE PROBLEM

Over 40 years ago, China sent in 40,000 troops to occupy Tibet. Many people, including the Dalai Lama, the spiritual leader of Tibet, fled to India and are still living there. In 1987, Tibetans in Dharmsala, in northern India, demonstrated in support of anti-Chinese riots in Lhasa, the capital of Tibet.

The refugee situation in the world today is reaching a crisis point — the numbers of refugees have doubled in the last ten years alone. The organizations set up over 40 years ago to help them are no longer able to cope with the sheer size of the problem. Why is this happening?

THE NORTH-SOUTH GAP

In the big-spending 1970s, many poorer countries were encouraged by international banks to take out huge loans to finance their development. The idea was that they should "catch up" with the rich countries of the world. But over the years they had to pay higher prices for key products such as oil and machinery, while the sums they received from their own produce stayed the same or even dropped. Today, many of the world's poorest countries are crippled by international debts, and are unable to feed their own growing populations. In 1991, these countries paid out more money in debt repayments than they received in aid from the rich North.

The problem of debt is made worse by a rapidly increasing population. Most population growth is taking place in the developing countries, which is likely to result in more and more people being unable to feed themselves. One billion people in the world are hungry today — that is one person in five. This number will continue to rise as world population rockets from 5.1 billion today, to possibly 8.5 billion by the year 2050. As we have seen, poverty uproots people, who may flee their homes and come knocking on the doors of the rich countries of the North.

SUPERPOWERS AT WAR

Many of the wars that have taken place in the last 40 years have been encouraged by the world's most powerful nations. People have lost their homes and livelihood. Neighboring countries have had to carry a refugee burden they can ill afford. Opposing sides in wars in Ethiopia, Somalia, and the Sudan, for example, were backed by either the former Soviet Union or the Western powers in a struggle for power and influence in the area.

International aid may not reach the innocent victims caught in the crossfire of these conflicts. In a drawn-out civil war in Ethiopia, General Mengistu and his government diverted food aid to his own soldiers. He also increased the refugee problem by forcing villagers out of their homes and by spending large amounts of government money on a war against a section of his own population.

Sometimes the link between superpower ambition and a long-term refugee problem is more direct, for example when a superpower itself invades a neighboring country. Just over 40 years ago, Communist China invaded Tibet and imposed its own government on the people there. Many Tibetans fled to India and Nepal and have not returned to their home country since. More recently, in 1979, the invasion of Afghanistan by the former Soviet Union sent many Afghans fleeing across the mountains into Pakistan. Many paid their life savings to guides who smuggled them across the border. Thanks to the

These Afghani children, huddled around a plate of food, are among the 14,000 Afghans living in this refugee camp in Pakistan.

generosity of their hosts and fellow Muslims, they are not the poorest of the world's refugees. Yet half of all Afghan refugees are children who have never seen Afghanistan. Although Soviet troops withdrew from their country in 1989, no mass return has taken place since. Afghans are fearful of going back to houses and lands ruined after the ten-year war.

The Gulf War of 1991 was an international conflict of a rather different kind. What started as an invasion of the oil state of Kuwait by its neighbor, Iraq, grew into a short but shattering desert war that involved the armed forces of a number of Western countries, including the United States and Britain. People argue as to whether the West was defending the freedom of Kuwait as an independent state or simply fighting to recapture much of its valuable oil supplies.

The Iraqi invasion meant that wealthy Kuwaitis had to flee their country or risk death. It also destroyed the livelihood of many foreign workers in Kuwait from poorer countries such as India and the Philippines. These people lost everything. They waited for many weeks at overflowing refugee centers, often with little or no shelter, until arrangements could be made to transport them back to their countries of origin.

Long after the war itself was over and the Iraqi forces had been forced to withdraw behind their own borders, the lives of many civilians in the area were still shattered. The Kuwaitis began to return home to try to rebuild their country; but many ordinary Iraqis found that they were also refugees. Their homes had been destroyed by the war or by armed attacks from a government choosing this time to show its strength at home by cracking down on the human rights of sections of its own population. Many wait without hope in refugee camps in neighboring Iran. For them, the end of the war has brought neither victory nor freedom.

The Gulf War shows how people, places, and the world's resources are all interlinked — and that the resulting refugee situation is part of that pattern. It is not a problem that belongs to "another" part of the world.

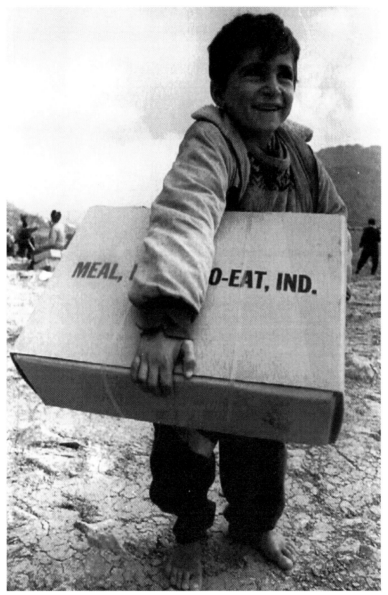

This Kurdish child is a victim of the Gulf War. He is one of thousands housed in camps along the Turkish border who relied on food rations dropped by U.S. military helicopters.

ATTITUDES AT HOME

As television programs have highlighted refugee stories across the world, it seems that attitudes in the democratic countries of the West are changing.

> Give me your tired, your poor, your huddled masses yearning to breathe free.
>
> *Emma Lazarus,*
> *Statue of Liberty inscription,*
> *New York*

Such attitudes were how refugees from Europe were once made welcome in the New World. But today, the old definitions of the word *refugee* are crumbling. The 1951 UN convention, which defined a refugee as a person with a "well-founded fear of being persecuted for reasons of race, religion, nationality, membership of a particular social group or political opinion," was intended to apply to Europeans after World War II, although in 1967 it was extended to refugees in other parts of the world. Its creators never envisaged the exploding statistics of refugees now in transit throughout the world.

Definitions become blurred as people argue over whether refugees are "political," "economic," "environmental," or perhaps all three. The term *asylum seeker* is used more commonly now, meaning one who seeks a safe refuge.

International law recognizes the right of a person to seek asylum but does not oblige countries to provide it. Many "invisible refugees" exist, too, people who have been displaced within their countries because of war or eviction, but who are not registered as refugees by their governments or the UNHCR.

Desperation forces people to flee to the West illegally. Western countries still attract refugees because of higher living standards and the promise of freedom from persecution. The revolution in communications has made flight by air a popular choice for asylum seekers.

Countries protect themselves against the world outside through control of their borders. In the United States over one million people were arrested in 1990 trying to cross the Mexican border. Razor wire, dogs, helicopters, and police keep out the "illegal aliens," as the U.S. Immigration Service calls them, fleeing from El Salvador, Guatemala, Honduras, Mexico, and Nicaragua. Most of the migrants were Mexicans, of whom 15 were shot in 1990. Despite all the efforts of the border patrols, two out of three succeeded in their bid to reach the United States.

FORTRESS EUROPE

In 1991 the Communist government finally collapsed in the Soviet Union, and the country disintegrated into a commonwealth of independent republics. Here and in Eastern Europe, where communism was abandoned, old conflicts among different ethnic groups sometimes reappeared. In the case of Yugoslavia a bitter civil war broke out between the Serbians and Croatians.

In an atmosphere of uncertainty about the future, many people from Eastern Europe flocked to the West. The number of asylum seekers rose from 13,000 in 1972 to 420,000 in 1990, and nearly half of these came to Germany. Some groups have begun attacking foreigners, particularly guest workers, who they think take jobs from Germans.

Some 20,000 Albanians have fled to Italy since 1990 and the Italian government says it can absorb no more. In Switzerland, low-paid hotel workers have included asylum seekers from Yugoslavia, Turkey, and the Middle East. As a result of the world recession in 1990 and 1991, jobs became scarce and many immigrants were simply sent home.

Tamils fleeing civil war in Sri Lanka made news when they were turned away by British immigration officials in 1987. Ravi Sundralingam arrived with a forged passport and visa. His brother had already been shot in Sri Lanka and he had been tortured. When he was returned to Sri Lanka he was tortured again.

As the barriers fall within the European Community they are erected even higher against refugees from outside. Countries claim "ownership" of their citizens, to whom they grant passports as a privilege. Without a passport, no freedom of movement is possible, and the

When they saw the changes taking place elsewhere in Eastern
Europe, thousands of Albanians tried to escape the
oppression they still had to endure in their own country. In
1990, huge crowds of Albanian refugees scrambled onto
boats to escape across the Adriatic Sea to Italy.

state can deny or confiscate passports at will. Today,
airlines bringing passengers to Britain without valid visas
face severe fines; thus the government is asking airline
staff to operate as immigration officials. Asylum seekers
pay sums they often cannot afford to traders in forged

documents — up to $5,000 or $6,000 a head.

Europe's control of its borders is extremely efficient. Only 0.17 percent of the population of Western Europe is made up of refugees. As the North-South gap widens, the jealous countries of Europe are likely to become even more careful guardians of their wealth and privilege in **Fortress Europe.** New laws on immigration are under discussion in a number of European countries.

FINDING A WAY

As the poverty gap widens and the growing world population has unequal shares in the world's wealth, the refugee problem seems almost impossible to solve. But a start can be made if the rich countries of the North and the poor countries of the South act together to find solutions.

In the short term, the rich nations could support the relief organizations more generously. In the longer term, they could cancel the crippling debts and encourage development that is actually useful to the countries of the South and doesn't reduce them to mere providers of raw materials. There is also the constant need to improve and maintain human rights, which are still ignored and abused in many parts of the world.

Our willingness to tackle one of the greatest humanitarian challenges of this century is not only a test of our commitment to human rights and our belief in the fundamental worth of the human person; it is also a step towards building a better and safer world.

UN high commissioner for refugees, 1991

Refugees throughout the world share a common humanity. Any one of us might be suddenly forced to flee our home for reasons beyond our control. Then, like the Kurdish man who held out the body of his dead baby son to the cameraman who came to film him in the mountains of Kurdistan, we might also cry in pain: "Why? Why? Why has the world abandoned us?"

KEY DATES

1280 B.C.
Flight of a nation: Moses leads the Israelites from Egypt to seek the Promised Land of Palestine (Canaan).

A.D. 1214
War displaces people: Emperor Genghis Khan and Mongol army take Beijing and overrun China.

1685
First recorded use of the word refugee: Louis XIV forces French Protestants (Huguenots) to flee to England as *réfugiés*.

1780
First recorded use of word refugee in the United States: Applied to fleeing supporters of George III during War of Independence.

1838-1839
Expulsion of a people: "Trail of Tears" on which 4,000 Cherokee die when they are driven from their lands.

1921
Protection for stateless people: Nansen passport devised by Dr. Fridtjof Nansen, high commissioner for refugees, fails to protect refugees after World War I.

1948
Whose homeland? The state of Israel is created but in turn displaces the Palestinians, of whom 2.5 million become refugees.

1951
Definition of refugees: UN Convention on the Status of Refugees gives people the right to apply for asylum and show they are political refugees fleeing persecution. This definition, framed to protect European refugees after World War II, is expanded to apply to refugees worldwide in 1967.

1961
Keeping people in: Berlin Wall built to prevent East Germans from escaping to the West.

1972
Expulsion of an ethnic minority: Idi Amin expels 27,000 Ugandan Asians.

1975
Escape by sea: Following the fall of South Vietnamese capital Saigon to the Communists, Vietnamese, Cambodian, and Laotian "boat people" flee to Thailand and surrounding countries. They are labeled "economic" refugees.

1978
Drought and famine create refugees: People fleeing starvation because of drought in the Sahel are labeled "environmental" refugees.

1991
Rescue story: "Operation Solomon" transports Ethiopian Jews (Falashas) to safety in Israel.

GLOSSARY

asylum: Shelter and protection afforded by a host country to a refugee.

civil war: War between opposing groups inside a country.

diaspora: The scattering of a people throughout the world, usually as a result of war, persecution, or economic reasons.

economic refugee: Someone who is considered to be on the move not because of persecution but who simply seeks higher living standards afforded elsewhere.

emigrant: Someone who leaves one country to live permanently in another, for any reason.

ethnic minority: Group which differs in race (and possibly religion) from most of the population.

forced repatriation: Returning someone as a prisoner, by force, to his or her country of origin.

"Fortress Europe": Expression describing the current growing policy of European nations to tighten immigration policies and border controls to deter refugees from entering their countries.

guest workers: Immigrants, mainly from southern Europe, encouraged by governments in the 1960s and 1970s to fill job vacancies in northern Europe.

host country: The country that receives a refugee, either on a temporary or permanent basis.

human rights: Basic rights of all human beings, including freedom of personal beliefs and speech.

immigrant: Someone who settles in a new country having left his or her country of birth or origin.

integration: Fitting in with a local community, and the wider society of which it is a part.

"push and pull" factors: Reasons that drive people to flee, such as famine, persecution, and war, and attract them to a host country, such as religious freedom, jobs, and better living standards.

racist: Emphasizing differences or encouraging hatred between races or ethnic groups.

refugee: Someone forced to seek safety elsewhere, usually in a foreign country, in order to escape persecution or as a result of a national disaster.

screening: Questioning new arrivals in a country to find out more about them — for example, whether they are at risk in their home country.

stateless: Having no nationality or citizenship; in particular having no papers such as a passport or identity card as proof of nationality.

transit camp: Temporary camp in which a refugee awaits processing for resettlement in third country or return to country of origin.

visa: A permit issued by a country to people it allows in as visitors, or to its own citizens allowing them to leave.

INDEX